Stroll and Walk, Babble and Talk

For Mike and Sue Cleary—my first teachers
—B.P.C.

Synonym:
A word that has the same or nearly the same meaning as another word

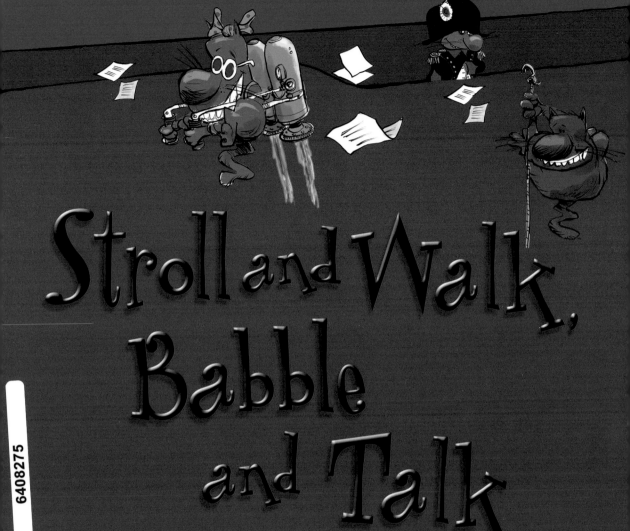

Stroll and Walk, Babble and Talk

More about Synonyms

by Brian P. Cleary

illustrations by Brian Gable

M MILLBROOK PRESS / MINNEAPOLIS

Whether you're moseying, strolling, or walking,

babbling,

chattering,

mumbling, or talking,

Synonyms help us
select the right word,

MAGIC SHOW

as in sly or clever,

and say what we mean,
like superb or terrific.

Your options for words
will quadruple—plus half—

When you start to use
all the words

that mean laugh.

Try giggle

and Snicker

and chuckle and chortle—

you get to choose what works best!

You might prefer crack up,

and (just as a backup)

you may think that cackle has zest.

Each SYNONYM has
quite a similar meaning,

like Washing
and Scouring,

scrubbing

and cleaning.

Synonyms sometimes will tell us degree.

Pick warm, hot, or steaming when you describe tea.

They give us

alternatives,

substitutes,

choices,

and help give our stories
more interesting voices!

Exit and leave,

lie and deceive,

funny and somewhat amusing.

Easy and simple,

a blemish or pimple—

just make up your mind
and start choosing!

Fast and quick,

ill and sick,

a greenback, a buck,
or a dollar.

Synonyms give you selection and choice.

They make you sound just like a scholar.

So pick among difficult,
hard, or demanding.

It needn't be
frightening
or scary.

Synonyms can help you to get or procure

a mighty big vocabulary.

Now go make your writing compelling, exciting, so thrilling

you might **brag** or **boast**.

One day, you'll fill bleachers,
When speaking to teachers—
you'll start with a synonym toast!

So, what is a SYNONYM? Do you know?

Find activities, games, and more at
www.brianpcleary.com

ABOUT THE AUTHOR & ILLUSTRATOR

Brian P. Cleary is the author of the best-selling Words Are CATegorical©
series, as well as the Math Is CATegorical©, Sounds Like Reading™, and
Adventures in Memory™ series, The Laugh Stand: Adventures in Humor, Peanut
Butter and Jellyfishes: A Very Silly Alphabet Book, Rainbow Soup: Adventures in
Poetry, and Rhyme & PUNishment: Adventures in Wordplay. Mr. Cleary lives in
Cleveland, Ohio.

BRIAN GABLE is the illustrator of several Words Are CATegorical© books, as
well as the Math Is CATegorical© series. Mr. Gable also works as a political
cartoonist for the Globe and Mail newspaper in Toronto, Canada.

Text copyright © 2008 by Brian P. Cleary
Illustrations copyright © 2008 by Lerner Publishing Group, Inc.

Millbrook Press
A division of Lerner Publishing Group, Inc.
241 First Avenue North
Minneapolis, MN 55401 U.S.A.

Website address: www.lernerbooks.com

Library of Congress Cataloging-in-Publication Data

Cleary, Brian P., 1959-
    Stroll and walk, babble and talk : more about synonyms / by Brian P. Cleary ; illustrated by Brian Gable.
        p.   cm. — (Words are categorical)
    ISBN 978-0-8225-7850-5 (lib. bdg. : alk. paper)
    1. English language—Synonyms and antonyms—Juvenile literature. I. Gable, Brian, 1949- ill. II. Title.
PE1591.C554 2008
428.1—dc22   2007040360

Manufactured in the United States of America
1 2 3 4 5 6 7 — JR — 14 13 12 11 10 09